Makerspace Careers™

T0030419

CAREERS IN

WELDING

MARY-LANE KAMBERG

Rosen
YA™
New York

For Kyle Ladewig

Published in 2020 by The Rosen Publishing Group, Inc.
29 East 21st Street, New York, NY 10010

Library of Congress Cataloging-in-Publication Data

Names: Kamberg, Mary-Lane, 1948– author.
Title: Careers in welding / Mary-Lane Kamberg.
Description: First edition. | New York : Rosen Publishing, 2020. | Series: Makerspace careers | Audience: 7–12 | Includes bibliographical references and index.
Identifiers: LCCN 2018052182| ISBN 9781508188162 (library bound) | ISBN 9781508188155 (pbk.)
Subjects: LCSH: Welding—Vocational guidance—Juvenile literature.
Classification: LCC TS227.7 .K36 2020 | DDC 671.5/2023—dc23
LC record available at https://lccn.loc.gov/2018052182

Manufactured in the United States of America

CONTENTS

INTRODUCTION

S ince ancient times, humans have been working to join metal pieces together for parts, products, construction, maintenance, and repair. In modern times, more than one hundred processes accomplish that goal by welding a wide variety of metals for a myriad of purposes. Along with welding, workers join metals using the related techniques of soldering and brazing. The wanted end product, types of metals used, and where the job will be performed contribute to the choice of method.

Because of America's trend toward new manufacturing and construction, as well as the need to improve infrastructure, including bridges, the job outlook for welders is good. In fact, because of the increased need for these skilled workers, along with the fact that many welders are reaching retirement age, experts agree that there is a shortage of qualified workers in the field.

That's why unions, trade schools, and others are recruiting more welder trainees. Recruiters are increasingly appealing to youth and women to fill the gap. Female welders filled shipyards and construction sites during World War II, when the vast majority of able-bodied men were busy fighting overseas. However, men dominate the ranks of today's welders.

Public access workshops known as makerspaces, Fab Labs, or hackerspaces are great places to learn the skills

Although welding has traditionally been a predominantly "male" career, more women are training to become welders. This is a welcome change since many qualified welders are reaching retirement age.

necessary to be admitted to apprenticeship programs. These venues offer access to tools, machines, and other equipment, as well as space to work on individual projects. Some makerspaces offer classes, as well as advice from other participants in a friendly, sharing environment.

The good news is that makerspaces are open to teens, who can start preparing for welding careers. High school technical education classes cover the basics. So young people can try their hands at welding to see if they like it and have an aptitude for it. Self-teaching opportunities include online videos and online classes.

For further instruction, potential welders can take classes at community colleges, private vocational schools, and union training centers to prepare for apprenticeship programs.

Practice is the best way to prepare for a welding career. And makerspaces can be used for that purpose, too. The goal is to be able to make the same types of welds over and over and have each look the same. That takes commitment and persistence over time.

Welders must be lifelong learners. New techniques, tools, and machinery constantly appear in the industry. So even trained welders need continuing education to stay up to date. Other tips for a successful career include supplementing training with additional certifications for different types of welds and specializing in a particular weld.

In this book, you'll learn what welding careers are like, as well as how to get started in the field, where to get additional experience, and how to find welding jobs. You'll also learn tips for presenting yourself in the best light on résumés and during in-person job interviews. You'll also get job outlook and other information from the Bureau of Labor Statistics.

CHAPTER ONE

WHAT IS WELDING?

Aaron McNeely likes to talk about his welding career as a boilermaker. "I do things people can't comprehend," said the welder from Clinton, Missouri. "They're shocked when I tell them about my job."

He wows friends with tales of the times he performed incredible feats in his welding jobs, including one in which he worked inside a metal box where the temperature was 160 degrees Fahrenheit (71 degrees Celsius). He impresses them with the story of the time he worked at a nuclear power plant surrounded by guards with assault rifles. He tells them about a fellow welder who had to work on a power plant smokestack 707 feet (215 meters) in the air.

"As a boilermaker, you have to be able to stand on your head and make an X-ray quality weld using a mirror," he said in an interview. An X-ray quality weld is one that

Although some welders work in machine shops, others work in the field, either indoors or outdoors in a variety of environments and weather conditions.

passes examination using an X-ray machine to see beneath the surface.

Welding is the process of using heat to join or cut pieces of the same metal. A blowtorch fires up. Sparks fly. A sizzling sound fills the air. And the temperature rises as welders shape metals into useful products. Not all welds use blowtorches. And some types of blowtorches create no sparks at all. But the image of workers wearing welding hoods as sparks fill the work space is what many picture when they think of welders.

Welding is an important skill that is in demand in construction, manufacturing, and other industries. Welders build ships, tankers, submarines, aircraft, cars, and locomotives. They also build and repair power plants, forge tools, and manufacture consumer goods. The US Department of Labor predicts employment in the field will increase 6 percent between 2016 and 2026, about the same as the average estimated growth for all jobs.

McNeely had no intention of pursuing a welding career. In college, he thought he'd like to be a teacher. He took up welding as part of his hobby driving in a demolition derby. Demolition derby is a motor sport in which drivers compete by purposely crashing their cars into each other. McNeely had his own welding machine and learned to use it to repair his demolition cars at home.

"I started college, but couldn't afford to continue," he said. "But I needed to make a decent living. A welding shop gave me a job even though I wasn't experienced. I took a welding test, and they saw potential."

Later, when he had more experience, he wanted to work in the field on job sites rather than in a shop. He attended a welding school in Tulsa, Oklahoma, and wanted to apply for an apprenticeship with the pipefitters union. An apprenticeship is a paid or unpaid supervised training period in which participants learn a trade. However, he learned that it would take six years. Instead, he applied to the International Brotherhood of Boilermakers, Iron Ship Builders, Blacksmiths, Forgers, and Helpers, one of the labor unions that represent welders. That union accepted him into its four-year program.

ALPHABET SOUP

Although there are as many as one hundred types of welding, four processes are the most common: gas metal arc

MUCH THE SAME

Welding is similar to brazing, soldering, and cutting, which are ways to use heat to fuse or separate metal. Brazers connect pieces of metal by heating and melting a metal alloy to use as a filler in the space between the pieces. An alloy is a mixture of two or more elements, including at least one metal created by melting them together.

The melting point of the filler must be lower than that of the metal being joined (otherwise the metal would melt, too). In addition to joining two pieces of the same metal, brazers can fuse pieces of different metals, including aluminum, silver, copper, gold, and nickel.

Sometimes brazers use flux to clean and protect metal. Flux is a substance that gains electrons when heated. Therefore, it reduces the oxidation of the metal, preventing rust. Flux is a liquid that helps filler run over the metal and helps it tightly bond to the metal pieces. Brazed pieces of metal are weaker than welded ones. But brazing is a good technique to use with cast iron and thinner metals that warp at the higher temperatures used in welding.

Like brazers, solderers use temperatures lower than welders use. Soldering also uses fillers—called solders—that melt below 840°F (450°C). Traditionally, lead was used as solder. However, environmental issues prompted the industry to use lead-free alternatives.

The solderer melts the solder and places it between the pieces of metal. As it cools and hardens, it bonds to the metal pieces and connects them. Solderers also

(*continued on the next page*)

(continued from the previous page)

use flux to clean metal and help the solder flow over the pieces to be connected. This process produces weaker joints than welding or brazing. Gold, silver, copper, brass, and iron can be soldered. This process is often used to connect electrical components using a conductive solder.

Soldering is similar to welding. It's often used to join metals like copper and iron, particularly in electronics.

Cutters use heat to cut or trim metal. Some use machines that resemble welding machines. Like welders, cutters sometimes use heat from an electric arc. They may also use ionized inert gas or burning gas. Cutters make metal pieces fit to specified measurements. They may also break apart cars, ships, railroad cars, buildings, or aircraft.

welding, gas tungsten arc welding, shielded metal arc welding, and flux cored arc welding. The kinds of welds are commonly called GMAW or MIG, GTAW or TIG, stick, and flux.

GAS METAL ARC WELDING

Gas metal arc welding (GMAW), also known as metal inert gas (MIG), is the most common industrial type of welding. It was first used in 1940 to join pieces of aluminum and other noniron metals. Today, it's used in the automotive and pipe industries, as well as in building and repairing bridges.

In this process, a metal wire electrode conducts electricity from direct current to create an electric arc in the presence of argon or helium. An electrode is a metal part that conducts electricity from a power source to an object, such as a piece of metal for welding. Argon and helium are inert gases that protect the weld from contaminating materials in the air. The arc heats the metals to melt and join them.

GAS TUNGSTEN ARC WELDING

Gas tungsten arc welding (GTAW) is also called TIG for "tungsten inert gas." It's most often used to weld thin pieces of stainless steel, magnesium, aluminum, and copper alloys. However, it can be used to weld any metal. Like GMAW/MIG, it uses an electric arc shielded by argon or helium to heat the metal. In this type of welding, the electrode is made of tungsten.

This method takes more time and is more complex than GMAW/MIG, and it requires more time to master. With GTAW/TIG, the worker inserts a filler metal between two pieces of metal. The intense heat of a welding torch melts the filler material and joins the pieces.

This type of weld is used in the aerospace industry to make space vehicles. It's also used in the bicycle and piping industries, as well as for maintenance and repair work. The equipment is not portable, so it's only used in welding shops.

SHIELDED METAL ARC WELDING

Shielded metal arc welding (SMAW) is a manual process also known as manual metal arc welding (MMAW), flux shielded arc welding, and most commonly, stick welding. It's another form of arc welding in which electricity creates an arc to heat filler material called slag used to join metal pieces. Slag is a by-product of smelting—removing a metal from ore. It can be a mixture of metal oxides and silicon dioxide, but in some cases it contains metal sulfides and pure metals.

Stick welding needs no inert gas shield. Instead, it uses flux to shield the metal from corrosion. SMAW is easy and efficient, as well as cost effective. It's most often used to

Welding is an important skill needed for joining metals in consumer and industrial manufacturing as well as construction, maintenance, and repair work.

weld copper, iron, aluminum, and nickel in industrial fabrication industries; to construct steel structures; and to weld cast iron (which is brittle) and ductile iron (which bends).

FLUX CORED ARC WELDING

Flux cored arc welding (FCAW), or flux welding, is used to weld thick pieces of metal, perhaps as thick as .25 inch (0.6 centimeters). This type of welding also uses flux to protect metal from contaminants. The method is portable and can be used outdoors. It's similar to MIG welding. In fact, it can be used on a MIG welding machine. The main difference is how the electrode is shielded. While the MIG process uses gas to protect the weld, the FCAW electrode is protected from the air using a hollow wire with flux in the middle. MIG is not recommended for windy or drafty conditions.

In some cases, the process needs dual shielding with gases such as carbon dioxide and argon or combinations of argon and oxygen or argon and carbon dioxide. Flux welding is often used in construction projects because of its speed and portability.

Welding techniques can be learned. No one is an expert starting out. "You can never be perfect," welder McNeely said. "You have to practice all the time. Once you can make the same type of weld over and over and all the welds look the same, you will start finding jobs."

CHAPTER TWO

HOW TO MAKE (ALMOST) ANYTHING

If you'd like to try your hand at welding but don't want to invest in equipment you may never use again, look for a makerspace. You can try out high-tech manufacturing machines. Some makerspaces provide welding machines, as well as classes and on-site help from trainers and other participants.

Members work on their own projects. They make objects for their own use, create prototypes for new products, or simply practice using the machinery. Some use the machines for arts or crafts projects. Others make or repair parts for bicycles or other equipment.

Makerspaces, Fab Labs, and hackerspaces support the trend toward STEM education (science, technology, engineering/design, and math). In present and future workplaces, employers need workers with knowledge and the skills to gather and evaluate information and solve problems.

Makerspaces have been around since at least 2005 and became loosely associated with *Make:* magazine when it was founded in 2011. They're often located in schools, libraries, or other facilities. Membership fees pay for machinery and operating costs. Makerspaces are often run as nonprofit organizations without formal affiliation with other similar spaces. Tools, equipment, and supplies vary widely from space to space. They are open to children and adults.

Fab Labs are similar to makerspaces. Both are collaborative community workshops that offer public access to equipment for making things. The main difference between them is similar to the differences between a family-owned hair salon and a Sport Clips haircut shop. A makerspace is independent. A Fab Lab is like a franchise. A franchise is a business opportunity that grants one party the right to use someone else's trademark, expertise, and business practices to sell products or services.

Founded in 2005 at the Massachusetts Institute of Technology (MIT) with a grant from the National Science Foundation, the first Fab Lab opened in Boston, Massachusetts. Fab Lab is a trademarked name for a network of work spaces that follow MIT's guidelines. A Fab Lab is officially affiliated with the MIT program.

Since 2016, at least 660 Fab Labs have sprung up worldwide in the United States, Canada, and Mexico, as well as South America, Europe, Africa, Asia, and Australia and New Zealand. They're found in bustling urban

WHAT'S IN A FAB LAB?

The official equipment list for Fab Labs shows the types of tools, machinery, and supplies available to participants. Not every Fab Lab has every item. And some have additional equipment. Whatever is there is available for use. This list shows the items available at the Fat Cat Fab Lab in New York City. Although this Fab Lab lacks welding equipment, it does have soldering machines. Other Fab Labs have welding machines and supplies.

Digital Fabrication:
- Desktop computers
- Laser cutter (80 Watt CO2)
- CNC router (CamMaster)
- Vinyl cutter
- 3D printer (large, medium, and small)

Electronics Tools:
- Soldering stations
- Oscilloscopes
- Power supplies
- Solder wick
- Solder paste
- Solder vacuum
- Flux
- Spare components (wire, capacitors, resistors, etc.)

Power Tools:
- Tabletop drill press
- Cordless drill
- Chop saw

(*continued on the next page*)

*(**continued from the previous page**)*

- **Jigsaw**
- **Router**

Hand Tools:
- **Screwdrivers**
- **Wrenches**
- **Ratchets**
- **Allen key sets**
- **Scissors and razors**
- **Glass cutters**
- **Chisels**

Electronics Equipment:
- **Arduinos in many configurations (uno, mega, micro, flora, etc.)**
- **Raspberry Pi**

communities and remote villages, as well as in high schools, colleges, and community centers.

A hackerspace is a community-run nonprofit organization. It may also be called a makerspace or hackspace. It serves the same purposes as makerspaces and Fab Labs: offering hands-on experience with tools and machinery, as well as a chance to socialize and learn from other users.

The idea for a hackerspace started around 1995 in Germany. The first hackerspace was started by a group of computer programmers who shared the same space. They soon added electronic circuit design and manufacture, followed by physical prototyping. They added

TRY THIS!

Use welding skills to create a simple pencil holder. All you need are a welder, a bench vise, files, a wire brush, a hacksaw, a sheet of 12-gauge steel, 10.5 inches (27 cm) of square steel tube with inner dimensions of .375 inch (1 cm) or larger, a magnet, and, of course, safety equipment. If you want to paint the finished project, add a can of spray paint. For the base, cut a rectangle from the steel sheet, 1.5 inches (3.8 cm) by 3 inches (7.6 cm), and file the edges smooth.

Students can learn and practice welding techniques in maker-spaces, private trade schools, and high school or community college vocational classes.

(*continued on the next page*)

*(**continued from the previous page**)*

The holders for the pencils are made from the steel tube. Cut it into four sections. You can make them all the same height or cut them in descending order starting with 3 inches (7.6 cm) and making each of the next three sections .25 inch (.6 cm) shorter than the one before. File both ends of each tube so they're smooth and stand straight.

Center the tubes on the base the way you like. You can cluster them or arrange them in a straight line. Hold them in place with a magnet. Use a tack weld to attach each side of the tubes to the base. Clean the welds with a wire brush and files. If you like, paint the finished product.

classes and access to equipment and charged membership fees to fund themselves.

You can participate in a makerspace with little or no technical knowledge. Trainers offer brief instruction on the use of the available equipment. And you can ask other users for tips and tricks.

Welding projects you can make in a makerspace include just about anything you can make from metal. Some participants simply enjoy crafting hobbies. Others are there to learn skills that can lead to future careers.

Start with a few simple projects. Work your way up to more involved objects, like fire pits and coatracks. After plenty of practice, you can take on even bigger projects, like barbecue grills or smokers or even a Formula Vee race car. You could try making a bench or table or cart. To find ideas, search the internet by entering "welding projects" in your browser.

Keep a record of each project, including the materials, machines, and tools used, in case you want to make it again. Keep notes of adjustments to try for future projects. Experiment with different types of welds and different tools and machines. Take photos of the finished projects, including close-ups of your welds. This file may come in handy when applying for an entry-level job or apprenticeship.

WELDING AS ART

This artist used welding and old bicycle parts to create this metal wall hanging art in Germany.

Challenge your creativity with art projects made from metal. You can make a wall clock, TV tray, coffee table, or other decorative pieces for the home. For instance, Ben and Kate Gatski created a ram's head to hang on the wall as an example of "green taxidermy." The piece is made of steel from reclaimed farm equipment. The sculptors cut, hammered, and welded the head. They then sealed it with water-based enamel.

Jason Tucker, who runs a plasma cutting and welding shop called Devlin Metal Works in Fort Frances, Ontario,

Canada, created a 4-foot-tall (1.2 m) metal moose as a custom sculpture for a customer's landscaping. He used TIG welds for the sculpture and stick-welded two pieces of steel rebar to two of the legs so the art object could be mounted in the ground. He primed and painted the finished product brown.

Or you can create metal sculpture for art's sake. For example, the Museum of Art in Fort Lauderdale, Florida, displayed a 5-foot-long (1.5 m) shark during its shark exhibition. Artist Stuart Peterman built the sculpture from hand-hammered stainless steel using a wire feeder welder.

The Nelson-Atkins Museum of Art in Kansas City, Missouri, has several metal sculptures on display in its outdoor sculpture park, including two painted steel pieces: *Rumi*, by Mark Di Suvero, and *Tom's Cubicle*, by Alexander Calder.

IN SEARCH OF MAKERSPACES

Where can you find and get involved in a makerspace? It's as easy as entering "find a makerspace" along with your location or "near me" into your web browser. You can also check with schools, libraries, and community centers in your area. Also check with organizations and websites that encourage participants who want to learn to weld, such as the following:

- American Welding Society Foundation
- Hackerspaces.org
- United States Fab Lab Network
- The Maker Directory

Finding a makerspace, hackerspace, or Fab Lab close to you is as easy as a Google search. When you find one (or more), visit its website to learn more.

Once you find a worker space, visit its website or call to see whether it has welding equipment to suit your needs. See if there is a trainer available to help you use the tools and machines. Learn how to join and find out whether you'll pay initiation fees or membership dues. Check to see if the days and hours the space is open fit your schedule.

Visit the space in person. See the equipment and discuss the kinds of projects you'd like to do. Ask whether other members know how to weld and whether they're likely to share their knowledge. Know that once you decide on a project, you must provide your own materials.

Finally, understand your own role in a makerspace, Fab Lab, or hackerspace. First, never endanger other users or damage equipment. Learn safety measures and emergency procedures. Learn where the fire extinguisher is and how to operate it. Keep your personal working area clean, and be sure to help clean the machines you use, as well as the rest of the work space.

CHAPTER THREE

ON THE JOB

Because welding creates a strong bond between metal parts, it's used in a wide variety of industries. According to the US Department of Labor, more than 60 percent of welders work in manufacturing. The rest are spread among shipbuilding, automobile repair, motor sports, aerospace, and construction

Welders help repair and maintain structures like the Brooklyn Bridge in New York City, as well as buildings and pipelines.

and repair of bridges, buildings, pipelines, power plants, and refineries. The particular metals being joined and the environmental conditions determine which kinds of welds are used. Welders need to be able to perform different types of welds.

On the job, welders' duties include studying blueprints or specifications, determining the dimensions of the parts to be welded, inspecting structures and materials, igniting torches or starting power supplies, monitoring temperatures to avoid overheating, and maintaining machines and other equipment.

AN ANCIENT SKILL

Welding dates from ancient times. Humans have been joining metal together at least since the Bronze Age (3700 to 500 BCE), when artifacts included small gold boxes created with pressure welds. In the Iron Age (1200 to 600 BCE), Egyptians welded pieces of iron together. During the Middle Ages (500 to 1500 CE), blacksmiths were welders. They used iron tools and hot fire to melt metals and hammer them together.

In 1800, British chemist and inventor Sir Humphry Davy created a battery-operated tool that produced an arc between carbon electrodes. In 1836, Davy's cousin Edmund Davy, also a British chemist, discovered acetylene, a compound of carbon and hydrogen. The gas was soon used in acetylene welding machines. In 1880, carbon arc welding began when scientists in the Cabot Laboratory

WHERE WELDERS WORK

Some welding jobs last only weeks or months. Travel to jobs is likely. Welders may move around for the same employer or different employers. Welders may find work in manufacturing, maintaining, or repairing some of the following products and entities:

- Automobiles, trucks, and motorcycles
- Metal parts for agriculture, mining, landscaping, and telecommunications equipment
- Boilers, tanks, and shipping containers
- Gas pipelines and oil rigs and pipelines
- Aboveground pipelines for oil, gasoline, natural gas, water, and electric utilities
- Military weapons, buildings, and vehicles
- Oil and gas refineries
- Chemical plants
- Power plants
- Robotics
- Military, cargo, research, cruise line, and passenger ships
- NASCAR and other motor sports pit crews
- Buildings, bridges, and civil engineering projects
- Repair, part making, or resurfacing of bulldozers and other heavy equipment for excavation, earth moving, and mining

in France used heat from an arc to fuse lead plates. The technique was also used to weld iron. Seven years later, gas welding and cutting came into use with the production of a blowpipe, or torch.

In the early 1900s, the invention of a coated metal electrode led to the creation of stick welding. About the same time, a torch that could be used with low-pressure acetylene was introduced. In the 1920s, research sought to find ways to shield the arc and welding area from environmental effects by using gases such as oxygen, nitrogen, hydrogen, helium, and argon.

Since then, new discoveries and inventions have made their marks on the welding industry. Gas tungsten arc welding was perfected in 1941, followed seven years later by shielded metal arc welding. Flux welding was invented in 1957. The newest techniques today include friction welding, created in the Soviet Union (now Russia), and laser welding, developed by Bell Telephone Laboratories. Over the years, new discoveries and methods have resulted in as many as one hundred types of welding. It's safe to expect continuing developments and improvements to welding processes in the future.

WORKING CONDITIONS

Most welders work full time and commonly work overtime. Those who work in manufacturing shops may have shift work for eight to twelve hours a day, which may include evenings and weekends. Those who work on job sites often work outdoors, including during bad weather. They may work on high scaffolding or platforms. Wages vary according to experience, skill level, and type of job.

Working conditions include outdoor sites in the heat of summer and dead of winter. This welder is working on a pipeline's insulation.

TAKE THE PLUNGE

Along with welding indoors and outdoors all over the world, some welders perform their jobs under the oceans and even in outer space. The biggest issue with underwater welding is the altered effect of gravity—the sense of weightlessness similar to what astronauts experience 220 miles (354 kilometers) above Earth.

Another important difference between welding on the surface and underwater is the danger involved. There are simply more ways to get hurt. Your lungs can expand and puncture if you hold your breath while swimming toward the surface—the same danger faced by scuba divers. Nitrogen bubbles in your blood can also get bigger as you swim upward and get stuck in your veins. Despite the risks, many welders work in shipping areas along the seacoasts and on oil rigs in the oceans.

Underwater welds are meant to be temporary until the objects can be fully repaired in a dry dock. Most submerged welds are stick welds, although in some cases, welders use flux and friction methods. They use waterproof electrodes with carbon steel or lighter metals.

LOST IN SPACE

With the privatization of space travel by companies such as SpaceX, Orbital Sciences, Blue Origin, Bigelow Aerospace, Space Dev, and Virgin Galactic, along with President Donald Trump's vision of a military space force, the need for welders who can make repairs and deal with emergencies in space is likely.

In fact, Soviet cosmonauts have already proved that welding works even in the cold depths of the cosmos. Georgi Shonin and Valeri Kubasov performed three types of welds during the *Soyuz 6* mission in 1969. The welds tested on stainless steel, titanium, and aluminum alloy using a Vulkan welding unit compared well to those performed on Earth.

More experiments were conducted in 1984 outside the Salyut 7 space station. Cosmonauts Svetlana Savitskaya and Vladimir Dzhanibekov showed that metal could be welded, cut, and soldered in a cold vacuum.

Today's space vehicles and stations are built with an eye to safety in the hopes that repairs will not be needed. The weight and bulkiness of welding equipment limit its use in the cramped confines of a spacecraft or space station. However, new equipment is available to mitigate those issues. For one, a compact handheld laser torch that is easy to use has been developed.

TOOLS OF THE TRADE

Because so many types of welds exist, the tools and machines needed for a welding career vary widely. Necessary hand tools include a grinder and hammer. Welders use grinders to make beveled edges or remove galvanizing from galvanized metal. Grinding pads give a smooth, seamless finish and make welds flush with the base metal. As welds are cleaned, a wire wheel removes slag, spatter, and discoloration.

Welders use hammers to line up seams of pieces of metal before welding. Hammers, too, remove spatter around welds and chip slag from stick welds. Hammers can also be used to fix distortion or stress from a finished weld. In addition to grinders and hammers, welders use a chisel

An angle grinder has a small disc that spins at a high rate of speed to remove rust or paint from metal, sharpen metal blades, or polish aluminum.

or chipping hammer to remove spatter. A chipping hammer has two edges on the head and a spring at the end of the handle. It's most often used to clean heavy slag from stick welds.

Welding machines differ depending on the type of weld they produce. Some are intended for certain types of welds. Others serve multiple purposes. The user can adjust voltage and amperage as needed. Complete welding systems include the welding machine itself, as well as power sources, monitors, and controllers. The power source may include a TIG gun, MIG gun, electrode holder, or other items with enough power to melt the metal to be welded. Monitors and controllers determine the quality of the weld or variations in the power supply for welds that require a consistent power supply.

PERSONAL PROTECTION

A career in welding can be hazardous to your health. According to the US Department of Labor, welders have one of the highest rates of illness and injury among all occupations. The two main dangers are burns and eye injuries. Exposure to hot materials can cause burns. It's common for welders to have pinprick scars from flying sparks on their arms and chests.

Intense light or hot slag and flying metal chips can cause eye damage. Ultraviolet light from a welding arc can cause burns or "welder's flash," also known as "arc eye." Welder's flash is a burn that affects the cornea and is similar to sunburn on the skin. The cornea is the clear, five-layer structure that covers the eye in front of the iris and pupil. It contributes to a person's focus.

Welders also risk electric shock. However, wearing protective gear and following safety procedures help minimize risks. Protective clothing includes a welding hood, fire retardant jacket, heat-resistant gloves, safety shoes or leather boots, goggles, and masks with protective lenses.

The Occupational Safety and Health Administration requires that welders' work environment be well ventilated so they can avoid inhaling gases or small particles that may fly into the air during the welding process. And, of course, having a fire extinguisher nearby is another important safety precaution.

CHAPTER FOUR

GETTING A HEAD START

I f you think you might like a career as a welder, you can start preparing while you're still in high school. Become familiar with the personal traits and skills welders need, and consider your own talents and personal characteristics.

For instance, welders need to be detail oriented to complete jobs that conform to specifications and are free from flaws. They also need to be neat freaks to clean grease and corrosion on welded surfaces and keep their work spaces clean and safe. They need a good sense of spatial reasoning. They should be able to work with employers and fellow tradespeople to coordinate tasks on job sites. And they must focus on the same task for long periods.

Welders need physical strength, endurance, and flexibility to lift heavy objects, work for a long time, and contort their bodies to bend, stoop, or stand to weld in difficult positions. Manual dexterity is a must. So are good eye-hand coordination and steady hands. Welders also need good close vision and depth perception to see delicate details in their work. They must be self-motivated and able to work on their own.

Eye protection is an important piece of safety gear when operating a blowtorch or other welding tools. In addition, protective clothing can minimize the risk of burns to the skin.

YOU'VE GOT PERSONALITY

Some students take personality tests to help them decide on a future career. One that has been proved scientifically valid and reliable is the Myers-Briggs Type Indicator, a self-reported questionnaire that indicates differences in how people see their world and make decisions. Results are classified into sixteen personality types.

Three personality types the Myers-Briggs test identifies as good fits for welding careers include the craftsman, the mastermind, and the architect. At the risk of mirroring the signs of the zodiac, test designers define these types as follows.

Craftsmen are artisans who like to see how mechanical objects work. They also like to troubleshoot and find the quickest way to solve problems. They are logical thinkers who are more interested in practical matters than theory. They're introverted, independent, and self-directed. They adapt well to change and work well in collaboration with others.

Masterminds also fall into the introvert category. They are analytical, intuitive thinkers, and good problem solvers. They look for innovative ways to improve procedures. They like the logical, predictable way mechanical objects operate. They also enjoy learning new information.

Like craftsmen and masterminds, architects are introverts who are interested in systems and designs. They enjoy theory as much as practical information. They're inventive and like to come up with their own ways to solve problems.

This type of testing should be only one of many considerations in choosing a career. Other personality types might also become good welders. For example, if you're the life of the party instead of an introvert, you can still become a welder. The most important trait is the desire to become a welder.

SKILL SETS

In addition to personality and physical traits, welders must master a number of skills to perform their jobs. These may include the following:

- Problem-solving skills
- The ability to read blueprints
- The ability to interpret sketches
- Understanding of two- and three-dimensional diagrams
- Math skills
- Computer skills, especially programming, to operate computer-controlled machinery
- Understanding of electricity
- Knowledge of metallurgy
- Familiarity with welding tools, equipment, and machinery
- Practical knowledge of different welding techniques
- Awareness of safety standards

CLASS ACTION

High school classes and activities can give future welders many of the skills they need. For example, courses in fine arts develop the characteristics of artisans. Classes in mechanical drawing and blueprint reading are also helpful.

Geometry, algebra, statistics, and precalculus contribute to a welder's ability to estimate costs and calculate dimensions. Physics contributes to knowledge of mechanical movement and electricity. Chemistry provides instruction in the properties of metals and their interaction with other elements in compounds for alloys. Physical education, weight

The ability to read and interpret sketches and blueprints is an important skill for welders. So is the ability to work and cooperate with others toward a common goal.

training, and health education classes help students achieve the physical fitness required for welding.

Some school districts have classes dedicated to students interested in careers in high demand that require high-tech skills, including welding. For example, one school district in Kansas has a Technical Advanced Training Center that combines student interest, hands-on activities, and part-nerships with local industry. The two-year program is open to juniors and seniors for three hours each school day for classroom and lab instruction.

The center's welding program focuses on fabrication processes for manufacturing, and the lab has state-of-the art tools, machines, and other welding equipment. Students have the opportunity to earn certification from the American Welding Society as an entry-level welder by passing written and practical skills tests.

JOIN THE CLUB

Extracurricular activities can contribute to preparation for a career in welding. Competing on sports teams builds physical fitness and also gives students a chance to work together toward common goals and develop interpersonal skills. Look for school clubs and activities that apply to the skills you need to learn.

One national student association has local chapters in middle schools, high schools, and colleges and universities. SkillsUSA brings together students, instructors, and repre-sentatives of private businesses, industries, and labor unions to help prepare the high-tech workforce America needs.

The organization seeks to prepare youth for careers in trade, technical, and skilled service occupations. Founded in 1965, it has served more than 13.5 million members, according to its website.

Activities include hands-on projects, district and state conferences, and an annual national SkillsUSA Championship. Each championship offers competition in areas such as construction, information technology, leadership, and transportation. The manufacturing sector includes automated manufacturing technology, robotics and automation technology, and major appliance and refrigeration technology, among other areas that can include welding.

The US Department of Education has recognized SkillsUSA as "a successful model of employer-driven youth development training." See if your school has a chapter. If not, consider starting one.

DO IT YOURSELF

Look for additional opportunities outside of school. A part-time job can help you learn customer-service skills, as well as gain experience with workplace teamwork. For physical development, consider joining a private gym or joining a club sports team.

Makerspaces, Fab Labs, and hackerspaces offer opportunities to learn and practice welding skills. You'll benefit from a trainer's help when learning to use the tools and machines. Even if the space lacks welding equipment, you likely can try the similar processes of soldering or brazing. The work space may offer hands-on classes in addition to

Welders need to have all aspects of physical fitness: strength, endurance, and flexibility. Participating in athletics or joining a gym are good ways to achieve these traits.

public access to tools and equipment. You'll also have a chance to learn from fellow users and observe their projects and techniques. The more you practice, the better your skills will become.

Your self-taught learning process can also include videos and information from internet sources such as Weld

Guru, Lincoln Electric's resource page, Crown Alloys Company's general information page, and the more than 1,100 videos in Miller's welding video library.

INTERNET WELDERS

You can also check for interesting information from famous welders on the internet. Some of the more popular personalities include ChuckE2009, Colin Furze, Wyatt Swaim, and Jody Collier.

Although ChuckE2009 admits to a lack of extensive formal training and experience, his YouTube channel was among the first dedicated to welding. He posts videos of various projects on a variety of metals, primarily steel, aluminum, and cast iron. Some posts review the latest welding gear, machines, and accessories. Although there is some controversy concerning his qualifications, he has inspired many beginning welders, based on user comments on his site.

Colin Furze considers himself an inventor, not an "official" welder, but he uses extensive welding skills to create homemade hoverbikes and other vehicles, along with crazy inventions such as a high-voltage ejector bed to get him up in the morning and a scorching-hot toasting knife that cuts bread and toasts it at the same time. There are no instructional videos or reviews of products on his channel, but even newbie welders enjoy his antics.

Wyatt Swaim, also known as Mr. TIG, is a leading expert on TIG welding with more than thirty years' experience. He has worked on aircraft and has trained welders. He is one

Colin Furze uses welding techniques on many of the inventions he demonstrates in his YouTube videos.

of the trackside welders in pit crews at the Indianapolis 500 automobile race at the Indianapolis Motor Speedway. His videos about TIG welding include topics such as welding basics, welding tips and tricks, and TIG welding aluminum.

Jody Collier is another internet welding master. His experience includes more than thirty years spent welding pipe at nuclear power plants, coal-fired plants, and paper mills, as well as serving as a welding instructor for Delta Air Lines. His how-to videos include projects using TIG, MIG, and stick welding, along with equipment reviews, safety tips, and more.

For more formal education, consider online courses from the American Welding Society. You can learn at your own pace with seminars available on the American Welding Society website. The society's classes were developed and are continuously updated by senior American Welding Society instructors. Choose from options such as welding fundamentals, safety in welding, fabrication math, metallurgy, understanding welding symbols, and more.

CHAPTER FIVE

BROTHERS AND SISTERS

During the nineteenth-century Industrial Revolution in Great Britain and the United States, the first labor unions formed to protect workers' rights. A labor union is an organization of wage earners or salaried employees in a particular trade. Unions were founded during a period of low wages, long hours, and unsafe work environments.

Today, unions still seek to protect and further

Union workers march in the annual Labor Union Parade on May 1, 1911, in New York City.

members' rights and interests, such as wages, benefits, and working conditions. Unions negotiate contracts, advocate in government affairs related to members, and offer job training and access to job openings, among other benefits. They also provide training programs for helpers, apprentices, and journeymen.

Helpers are paid or unpaid welders' assistants. They lift and move tools and supplies; hold workpieces or clamp them to a table; remove impurities such as slag, rust, or grease; and perform other duties. Some helpers become welders. Others enjoy the occupation itself. Journeymen are skilled workers who have served an official apprenticeship and are qualified to perform a particular trade or craft without supervision.

Some advantages of union membership include higher wages, better benefits, and better contracts than those of nonunion workers. For example, according to the Bureau of Labor Statistics, in the decade from 2001 to 2011, union members earned an average of 28 percent higher wages than nonunion workers.

Union workers' employer-sponsored benefits also tend to be better than nonunion workers'. Union members get better medical benefits for themselves and their families and pay less of the cost for them. Union workers also get more paid sick days and vacation days, as well as better retirement benefits.

Unions stand behind workers who are at risk of being fired. In most states, nonunion workers can be fired at will. That means they can lose their jobs for nearly any reason (except for cases that involve legally defined exceptions for discrimination or whistle-blowing).

Whistle-blowing is the reporting of illegal or unethical information or practices within a private or public organization. By law, a whistle-blower cannot be fired simply for revealing negative facts or activities about an employer. On the other hand, union workers can be fired only for just cause. Just cause involves misconduct or disciplinary issues. Even in these cases, union members are usually entitled to a review process before losing their jobs.

Union workers have more clout in employer-employee contract negotiations for wages and working conditions than nonunion members. The strength in numbers encourages employers to make agreements that benefit their employees.

THE DOWNSIDE OF UNIONS

The drawbacks of joining a union mean that some welders choose not to join one. For instance, union members must comply with the decisions of the majority. If a majority of union members calls for a strike over contract disputes, all members must stay home from work. If a strike lasts too long, workers can suffer financial losses. If workers cross picket lines to continue working, striking workers call them scabs. The meaning of the term ranges from seriously unfriendly to hostile.

At the same time, most states let unions contribute to political lobbying efforts and endorse political candidates. That means that some of a worker's money goes to support these activities, even if the individual disagrees on an issue or supports different candidates.

In a unionized environment, seniority is more important than an individual's particular qualifications. Seniority is a privileged status that is based on the amount of time someone has been a member or worked at a specific job or for a specific employer. If a company must lay off workers due to declining revenue or seasonal work, those with the least seniority go first.

In some ways, union membership discourages employers from considering an individual's education, training, and experience in favor of seniority in decisions about promotions or transfers. And raises are determined by union contracts, not how hard or how well an individual works.

Also, union membership isn't free. Joining often requires initiation fees and ongoing monthly membership dues, usually based on a percentage of the member's income.

BOILERMAKERS, IRONWORKERS, AND PIPEFITTERS

Because of the wide variety of jobs welders do, they belong to different unions depending on the specific types of welding and types of employers. For example, some American and Canadian welders belong to the International Brotherhood of Boilermakers, Iron Ship Builders, Blacksmiths, Forgers, and Helpers, frequently called the boilermakers union.

First organized in 1880, this union serves more than two hundred locals in North America. A union local is a chapter, branch, or lodge affiliated with a national or international union.

Members build, maintain, and repair gas, coal-fired, and nuclear power plants, as well as refineries, paper mills,

Welders who work on gas-fired industrial power plants often belong to the International Brotherhood of Boilermakers, Iron Ship Builders, Blacksmiths, Forgers and Helpers.

and steel mills. You'll find them working in shipyards and on railroads, as well as mining coal, gypsum, and talc. They also manufacture tools and consumer goods. Boilermakers have worked on projects such as machinery to build the Panama Canal; the USS *Nautilus* nuclear submarine; the Gateway Arch in St. Louis, Missouri; and the aluminum-based fuel for the space shuttle's solid rocket boosters.

Welders may instead belong to the ironworkers union, formally known as the International Association of Bridge, Structural, Ornamental and Reinforcing Iron Workers. Ironworkers worked on major projects such as the Golden Gate Bridge in San Francisco, the Sears Tower in Chicago, and the World Trade Center and the Freedom Tower in New York City. They also work in shops.

Another union for welders is the United Association of Journeymen and Apprentices of the Plumbing and Pipe Fitting Industry of the United States and Canada, often known as the UA or the pipefitters union. It represents welders who work on pipes of all kinds: pipes that carry water, steam, gases, oil, and other materials.

Specialized welders known as journey wiremen in the United States and Canada belong to the International Brotherhood of Electrical Workers. Wiremen are electricians who perform tasks such as connecting business facilities and residences to an outside power source and distributing electricity throughout the structure. They may install, inspect, or repair lighting fixtures, electrical outlets, electric motors, alarm systems, electrical control panels, and computer networking and cable television systems.

Still other welders called millwrights belong to the United Brotherhood of Carpenters and Joiners of America, often called the carpenters union. Millwrights work in industries such as automotive, aerospace, food processing, pharmaceuticals, and more. Like boilermakers, they can be found at work in power plants.

RIGHT-TO-WORK STATES

Some states and US territories have right-to-work laws, which allow employees to work without joining a union. In Alabama, Arizona, Arkansas, Florida, Georgia, Guam, Idaho, Indiana, Iowa, Kansas, Louisiana, Michigan, Mississippi, Nevada, North Carolina, North Dakota, Oklahoma, South Carolina, South Dakota, Tennessee, Texas, Utah, Virginia, and Wyoming, workers benefit from union-negotiated wages and working conditions without having to join a union.

In some other states, workers may have to join a union before taking a job. Or they must join within a specified time after taking a job. In states without right-to-work laws, workers may have to pay a reduced portion of union dues even if they don't become members. Those fees compensate the union for negotiating contracts and other services, but none of that money goes to support political candidates.

SISTERS IN THE BROTHERHOOD

Although the welding industry is currently dominated by men, the number of women in welding is increasing. Maria

WINNIE THE WELDER

During World War II, women represented by the icon Rosie the Riveter worked in American factories and shipyards. Working alongside Rosie was another symbolic worker known as Winnie the Welder. With most able-bodied men serving in the military overseas, women stepped up to fill the critical jobs traditionally held by men.

Female welders worked building ships, submarines, vehicles, aircraft, and other items to supply the armed forces. By 1943, sixteen million women made up more than 50 percent of American workers, according to Kenton Anderson in the article "Winnie the Welder: Female Welders of WWII," posted on the Welding Supplies from IOC website. Twenty-five percent of them worked in shipyards. By 1945, women also made up one-third of the workers building B-29 bombers.

Holt of Portland, Oregon, wanted a job with hands-on, creative, physical work. When a friend went into welding, Holt thought she'd give it a try, too. She enrolled in a vocational training program. Out of her class of forty men and ten women, thirty-nine men passed, but she was one of only three women who did.

"Well, the union wasn't willing to take me, because my high school transcripts didn't quite qualify," Holt told the Fabricator magazine. "But the apprentice coordinator

As the demand for qualified welders to work on the nation's infrastructure and manufacturing increases, women are entering a field currently dominated by men.

called me and told me the ironworkers union in California wanted me to take pre-apprentice training."

She enrolled in the Gladiator Women Program, which was created especially for women. It's a class to prepare women for union apprenticeship programs. The first three-week session was held in 2015, with nine hours of class each day, six days a week. A second session was completed in 2016, and the program scheduled two more in 2017.

"We entered some awesome competitions," Holt said. "I got first place in a couple."

After completing her training, she got a TIG welding job in Portland. "I love it, I really do," she said. "I get to work with my hands, and the money is great."

Current and anticipated future needs for more welders to rebuild American infrastructure and fill manufacturing and other jobs have employers trying to recruit women to fill the gap. Around 2008, many employers tried to recruit women to the industry. Recruiters emphasized high pay and job stability and offered scholarships for training. But, they had little success. And some women who accepted the challenge and became welders experienced sexual harassment on job sites.

By 2018, new recruiting methods included classes for women taught by women. These classes often include sexual harassment training. Some programs that prepare women for entry-level welding jobs include Women Who Weld, Latinas Welding Guild, Weld Like a Girl, and the Gladiator Women Program.

CHAPTER SIX

GETTING THE JOB AND GETTING AHEAD

You can become certified as a welder at any age, as long as you have a high school diploma or the equivalent. More important than age is hands-on experience. You can get that in makerspaces and technical education classes in high schools and community colleges, private welding schools, union training centers, and the US armed forces or through the American Welding Society.

Some employers are willing to train entry-level

Learning to weld is only part of becoming a welder. Welders must practice to master it.

workers on the job. However, most prefer certified welders or at least those who have had some training. In fact, some pay for training and certification programs for new welders. Even with formal training, you can still expect to need several months of on-the-job training.

CERTIFICATION AND LICENSURE

To earn welder certification, look for a class or apply for a union apprenticeship. Or apply for a job at a local welding company that is willing to train you. Once you have some experience, sign up for the American Welding Society test for the certified welder credential at an accredited test center. You'll find one at a vocational school or union training center.

The test has no prerequisites. It's simply a hands-on test to demonstrate welding skills. However, there is no universal, one-size-fits-all exam. Certification shows that a welder has demonstrated a particular type of weld in a particular position using the American Welding Society's approved process. So welder certification reflects skills according to welding codes.

Each code applies to industries such as automotive, aerospace, manufacturing, oil drilling, oil refining, pipelines, and more. The types of welds certified depend on which metal and welding technology is used as well as the intended use of the product. For example, welders might demonstrate a particular type of weld on a plate, pipe, or boiler made of structural steel, sheet metal, aluminum, or stainless steel of various thicknesses. And they might perform the process in a vertical, horizontal, flat, or over-head physical position. Different employers require different certifications for different purposes, so you can work as a welder without passing every possible certification test.

Certification must be renewed every six months. To renew, welders submit documents from employers saying the welder is still working in the field and doing the same welding processes. In some states, welders need both certi-fication and licensure. And some cities require licenses for welders who work for the local government.

JOB SEARCHES

Some welders work for a single employer, particularly in manufacturing roles. Others move from job to job as required tasks are completed. For instance, Clinton, Missouri, welder Aaron McNeely is a journeyman welder. He and his younger brother, who followed him into the boilermakers union apprenticeship and also became a journeyman welder, travel together to jobs around the country, usually at coal-fired power plants. His jobs have taken him to Iowa, Kansas, and Minnesota.

Rather than working for a single company, he bounces from place to place, according to the needs of different employers. "I don't stay at one job very long," he said. "Every job has an end date. I enjoy the constant change, seeing new things and meeting new people."

McNeely's work is seasonal because maintenance and repair on power plants is scheduled during the times of year when the demand for electricity is lowest. He doesn't mind being off part of the year. "I make enough during the seasonal work that I can afford not to work during peak times," he said. "And I enjoy spending time with my family."

FINDING A JOB

Some employers who need welders simply call the appropriate union and say how many welders they need for which kinds of welds, materials, or other criteria. The union then contacts members in a predetermined order based on how recently they got hired through the union. Or the union posts openings on the union's website.

Nonunion welders can search the internet for jobs by entering "jobs, welders" and the city or state they want to work in. They can also search websites such as Indeed, Simply Hired, ZipRecruiter, or Monster. Welders can also learn about openings through their community college or private vocational school. Another way to find a job is by networking with makerspace friends, fellow students from a training program, or friends and family.

Before applying for a job, it's a good idea to prepare a résumé. A résumé is a document that summarizes a job candidate's education, qualifications, and personal and professional experience. Make a separate document for each job you apply for.

Every job needs welders with specific skills. Review the job posting to learn what the employer is looking for. Then highlight your skills, certifications, and experience in terms of those needs.

If you have experience with similar jobs, list them first. Some employers want to see past experience in

Welding jobs are often listed on labor union websites, as well as employment websites like Indeed.com. Schools and training centers can also assist in the job hunt.

chronological order (usually from most recent to oldest). However, if you want the job, don't make interviewers search your document for what they want to see. Instead, choose skills that are important to the employer and give examples of where you used those skills.

For instance, if blueprint reading is an important skill for a particular job, give an example of a previous job in which you used that skill. Add a comment about how your work contributed to the resulting project. Be sure to use the keywords "blueprint reading" in your explanation. The interviewer can pick them up on a quick scan of your document.

If you have little experience, list your education, training, and certifications first. Keep in mind that everything on the résumé must be true and accurate. If you claim to have a specific skill and don't, your welds will show it, and you won't be working at that job long.

FACE TO FACE

When you get a chance for an interview for a welding job, prepare yourself. Print a few copies of your résumé and review it so you're familiar with how you described yourself. Plan ahead for transportation to the interview and try to arrive about ten minutes early. Wear the clothes you would wear on the job. Remember, you should be prepared to perform a welding test.

During the interview, look the interviewer in the eye and smile before you answer questions. Be sure your body language shows that you're confident in your ability to serve the employer's needs. Ask your own questions during the

KEYWORDS AND PHRASES FOR WELDERS' RÉSUMÉS AND INTERVIEWS

Your résumé will pass the "scan" test if you include some keywords and phrases that are important in welding jobs. Choose from some of these when describing your experience on past jobs or during your training. It's also good to slip them into your answers when you're interviewed on the phone or in person.

- Calculating dimensions
- Interpreting sketches
- Reading blueprints
- Spatial reasoning
- 2D and 3D diagrams
- Clean work area
- Detecting changes in molten metal flows
- Following directions
- Identifying the characteristics of a joint
- Inspecting parts and materials
- Strictly abiding by safety standards
- Able to stoop, bend, reach, or stand for long periods
- Excellent close vision and depth perception
- Lifting considerable weight
- Manual dexterity
- Physical stamina
- Physical strength
- Steady hands
- Working in adverse conditions

(*continued on the next page*)

(continued from the previous page)

- **Documenting work**
- **Keeping supply inventory**
- **Meeting deadlines**
- **Organizing**
- **Planning**
- **Prioritizing**
- **Reliability**
- **Time management**
- **Teamwork**
- **Communication**
- **Working independently**
- **Self-directed**
- **Learning new technologies**
- **Operating (specific tools and machinery)**
- **Selecting and using grinders and other metal finishers**
- **Using lifting and control devices**

Source: Balance Careers.

interview so it's more like a conversation than an interrogation. Finally, ask for the job. Many candidates are too shy or fear rejection too much to ask, "May I have the job?"

If you're not hired on the spot, be sure to follow up with the interviewer. Dash off a text message or email expressing thanks for the interview, as well as your continued interest in the job. Follow up within a reasonable time if you hear nothing.

BOOSTING YOUR INCOME AND OPPORTUNITIES

Even if you like the type of welding you're doing, you can increase your income and qualify for more openings by following three steps for a successful career. First, work to increase your understanding and proficiency of your craft. Continue to practice your skills and strive to do your best at each job and on every weld.

Second, keep learning. Stay up to date on the latest tools, machinery, and other equipment. The best welders

Learning to weld is a lifelong process. Successful welders stay up to date on the latest innovations and learn new or advanced techniques to increase their value to employers.

are lifelong learners. They're always ready to try new processes, as well as increase their general knowledge of the industry. One way to learn is to teach others. Be willing to share your knowledge with less experienced welders. And ask those with more experience for their advice.

Third, grow your skills and experience. Because so many types of welding exist, the more you have mastered, the more qualified you are for the variety of welding jobs out there. On the other hand, specialization may prove to be your road to success. Some welding processes need additional education and specialized testing. For example, welders who work in chemical plants or oil refineries must meet higher standards. So must those who mostly work with sheet metal.

With skills that may have begun in high school classes or makerspaces, you can enjoy a successful, satisfying welding career.

GLOSSARY

alloy A mixture of two or more elements, including at least one metal, created by melting them together.

apprenticeship A paid or unpaid training period under supervision in which a worker learns a skilled trade or craft.

at will Describing a workplace environment in which employers can fire workers for nearly any reason, except for cases of discrimination or whistle-blowing.

chipping hammer A specialty hammer with two edges on the head and a spring at the end of the handle, used to remove slag from welds.

electrode A metal part that conducts electricity from a power source to an object, such as a piece of metal for welding.

flux A substance that gains electrons when heated. This process reduces the oxidation of the metal, preventing rust.

franchise A business opportunity that grants one party the right to use someone else's trademark, expertise, and business practices to sell products or services.

helper A paid or unpaid welder's assistant who performs tasks that require fewer skills than apprentices or journeymen have.

journeyman A skilled worker who has served an official apprenticeship and is qualified to perform a particular trade or craft.

just cause A legal reason for firing an employee that may involve misconduct or disciplinary issues.

labor union An organization of wage earners or salaried employees in a particular trade.

metallurgy The science of metals, including their properties, the separation of metal from ores, and the creation of alloys.

résumé A document that summarizes a job candidate's education, qualifications, and personal and professional experience.

right-to-work laws State laws that prohibit employers from requiring employees to join a union.

scab A worker who goes to work during a strike against an employer.

seniority A privileged status that is based on the amount of time someone has been a union member or worked at a specific task or for a specific employer.

slag A by-product of smelting—removing metal from ore. It can be a mixture of metal oxides and silicon dioxide, but in some cases it contains metal sulfides and pure metals.

union local A chapter, branch, or lodge affiliated with a national or international labor union.

welder's flash A burn from exposure to intense ultraviolet light that affects the eye's cornea. It resembles sunburn on the skin. Also known as arc eye.

whistle-blowing The reporting of illegal or unethical information or practices within a private or public organization.

X-ray quality weld A weld that passes examination using an X-ray machine to see beneath the surface.

American Welding Society (AWS)
8669 NW Street, #130
Miami, FL 33166-6672
(800) 443-9353
Website: http://awsnow.org
Facebook: @AmericanWeldingSociety
The AWS supports welders with certification, advanced
    training, standards, conferences, and information about
    career opportunities. It seeks to advance science technol-
    ogy and use of welding processes in the global community.

Canadian Welding Association (CWA)
8260 Park Hill Drive
Milton, ON L9T 5V7
Canada
(800) 844-6790
Website: https://www.cwbgroup.org/association
Facebook and Twitter: @cwbgroupwelding
The CWA is a Canadian nonprofit association that supports
    the welding industry. It offers a way for welders, employ-
    ers, fabricators, and welding product suppliers to
    exchange knowledge and resources. It also works with
    government and regulatory agencies to improve welding
    products and practices to advance welding careers.

Fab Foundation
50 Milk Street, 16th Floor
Boston, MA 02109
(857) 333-7777
Website: http://www.fabfoundation.org

Facebook: @fabfndn

Twitter: @FabFndn

The Fab Foundation is a nonprofit organization that grew out of MIT's Center for Bits and Atoms Fab Lab Program. It provides access for community organizations and schools to tools, information, and financial means to use digital fabrication to create opportunities to improve lives.

International Association of Bridge, Structural, Ornamental and Reinforcing Iron Workers

1750 New York Avenue NW, Suite 400

Washington, DC 20006

(202) 383-4800

Website: http://www.ironworkers.org

Facebook: @unionironworkers

Twitter: @TheIronWorkers

Commonly called the ironworkers union, the International Association of Bridge, Structural, Ornamental and Reinforcing Iron Workers is a labor union that represents welders, ironworkers, and workers in other trades associated with major construction projects.

International Brotherhood of Boilermakers, Iron Ship Builders, Blacksmiths, Forgers, and Helpers

753 State Avenue

Kansas City, KS 66101

(913) 371-2640

Website: https://boilermakers.org

Facebook: @boilermakers.union

Twitter: @boilermakernews

YouTube: International Brotherhood of Boilermakers
The International Brotherhood of Boilermakers, Iron Ship
    Builders, Blacksmiths, Forgers, and Helpers is a labor
    union that represents workers in heavy industry, ship-
    building, manufacturing, railroads, cement, mining, and
    other industries in the United States and Canada.

International Society for Technology in Education (ISTE)
1530 Wilson Boulevard, Suite 730
Arlington, VA 22209
(703) 348-4784
Website: http://www.iste.org
Facebook: @ISTEconntects
Twitter: @iste
Instagram: @isteconnects
The ISTE is a nonprofit organization of educators dedicated
    to using digital technology to improve teaching and
    learning. It serves as a network for educators and pub-
    lishes books and journals.

SkillsUSA
14001 SkillsUSA Way
Leesburg, VA 20176-5494
(703) 777-8810
Website: https:/www.skillsusa.org
Facebook, Instagram, and Twitter: @SkillsUSA
SkillsUSA is a national association of students, instruc-
    tors, and representatives of private industry with local
    chapters in middle schools, high schools, and col-
    leges and universities. Through local projects, state
    and district conferences, and national competitions,

it seeks to prepare youth for the high-tech workforce America needs.

United States Fab Lab Network
143 S. Jackson Street
Elkorn, WI
(262) 898-7430
Website: http://usfln.org
Facebook: @usfln
The United States Fab Lab Network is a group of Fab Labs
     that exchange information and resources to encourage
     people to experiment and invent new products.

UnLondon Digital Media Association
211 King Street
London, ON N6A 1C9
Canada
(226) 271-4753
Website: http://www.unlondon.ca
Facebook and Twitter: @unlondon
Describing itself as "Art + Make + Tech," the UnLondon
     Digital Media Association provides digital literacy edu-
     cation, an UnLab makerspace, workshops, and more to
     encourage use of digital technology.

FOR FURTHER READING

Christena, Stephen. *Learn to Weld: Beginning MIG Welding and Metal Fabrication Basics*. New York, NY: Crestline, 2014.

Farnsworth, Steven Robert. *Welding for Dummies*. Hoboken, NJ: Wiley Publishing, 2010.

Galvery, William. *Basic Welding for Farm and Ranch*. North Adams, MA: Storey Publishing, 2019.

Guyer, J. Paul. *An Introduction to Welding Structural Steel*. El Macero, CA: Clubhouse Press, 2017.

McDonald, Shawn. *Things You NEED to Know About TIG Welding*. Seattle, WA: Amazon Digital Services, 2017.

Morley, Jackson. *The TAB Guide to DIY Welding: Hands-On Projects for Hobbyists, Handymen, and Artists*. New York, NY: McGraw-Hill Education, 2013.

Parkinson, Peter. *Making Sculpture from Scrap Metal*. Ramsbury, Wiltshire, UK: Crowood Press, 2016.

Pearce, Andres. *Farm and Workshop Welding*. East Petersburg, PA: Fox Chapel Publishing, 2012.

Scott, Ralph Lee. *The Wilmington Shipyard: Welding a Fleet for Victory in World War II*. Mt. Pleasant, SC: History Press, 2008.

Uttrachi, Gerald. *Weld Like a Pro*. North Branch, MN: CarTech, 2015.

BIBLIOGRAPHY

Anderson, Kenton. "The History of Welding." Miller. Retrieved September 12, 2018. http://www.millerwelds .com/resources/article-library/the-history-of-welding.

Anderson, Kenton. "The Welding Way Back Machine." Welding Supplies from IOC, December 1, 2015. https://www.weldingsuppliesfromioc.com/wp/wp -content/uploads/2015/10/History-Of-Welding-V3.png.

Anderson, Kenton. "Winnie the Welder: Female Welders of WWII." Welding Supplies from IOC, April 21, 2017. https://www.weldingsuppliesfromioc.com/blog /winnie-the-welder-female-welders-of-wwii.

Bureau of Labor Statistics, US Department of Labor. *Occupational Outlook Handbook*, "Welders Cutters, Solderers, and Brazers." September 4, 2018. https:// www.bls.gove/ooh/production/welders-cutters -solderers-and-brazers.htm.

Clark, Audrey. "3 Traits Every Successful Welder Has." Arc-Zone.com. Retrieved October 20, 2014. https:// www.arc-zone.com/blog/carmenelectrode/2014/10/20 /l3-traits-every-successful-welder.

Danowski, Tom. "Women in Welding on the Rise." The Fabricator, January 11, 2017. https://www.thefabricator .com/article/arcwelding/women-in-welding-on-the-rise.

Decker, Fred. "Do AWS Welding Certifications Expire?" Chron. Retrieved October 16, 2018. https://work .chron.com/aws-welding-certifications-expire-10051 .html.

Doyle, Alison. "Welder Skills List and Examples." Balance
    Careers, July 7, 2018. https://www.thebalancecareers
    .com/welder-skills-list-2062500.
Farnen, Karen. "The Disadvantages of Being a Union Mem-
    ber." Career Trend, July 5, 2017. https://careertrend
    .com/info-7756905-disadvantages-being-union
    -member.html.
GoWelding.org. "FCAW Flux Cored Arc Welding."
    Retrieved October 13, 2018. https://gowelding.org
    /welding/FCAW-Flux-Coredc-Welding.
Kamberg, Mary-Lane. Creating with Laser Cutters and
    Engravers. New York, NY: Rosen Central, 2017.
Lombardo, Crystal. "13 Advantages and Disadvantages
    of Labor Unions." Vittana.org. Retrieved October 17,
    2018. https://vittana.org/13-advantages-and
    -disadvantages-of-labor-unions.
Long, George I. "Between Union and Nonunion Compen-
    sation, 2001–2011." Monthly Labor Review, April 2013.
    https://www.bls.gov/opub/mlr/2013/04/art2full.pdf.
Mraz, Stephen. "What's the Difference Between Solder-
    ing, Brazing, and Welding?" Machine Design, July 14,
    2015. https://www.machinedesign.com/basics-design
    /soldering-processes.
Nguyen, Oanh. "Personality Traits of a Successful Welder."
    Tulsa Welding School, August 7, 2015. https://
    weldingschool.com/blog/welding/personality-traits
    -of-a-successful-welder.
Rate My Welder. "Professional Welding: How to Become
    a Welder and How Much Do They Make?" Retrieved
    August 20, 2018. https://www.ratemywelder.com
    /professional-welding-how-to-become-a-welder-and
    -how-much-do-they-make.

Rate My Welder. "61 Cool Welding Project Ideas for Home, Hobbies, or to Sell." Retrieved August 20, 2018. https://www.ratemywelder.com/61-cool-welding-project-ideas-for-home-hobbies-or-to-sell.

Rease, C. L. "Tools Used in Welding." eHow. Retrieved October 16, 2018. https://www.ehow.com/about_5467371_tools-used-welding.html.

RodOvens.com. "Types of Welding Machines." March 28, 2015. https://www.rodovens.com/index.php/blog/types-of-welding-machines.

Welding Master. "Types of Welding Process—Everyone Should Know." November 3, 2017. http://www.theweldingmaster.com/types-welding-process.

Welding Schools. "Top 10 Qualities of a Great Welder." Retrieved October 17, 2018. http://weldingschools.com/resources/top-10-qualities-of-a-great-welder.

Wilkey, James. "Welding in Space." American Welding Society, July 22, 2015. https://awo.aws.org/2015/07/welding-in-space.

INDEX

ABOUT THE AUTHOR

Mary-Lane Kamberg is a professional writer specializing in young adult nonfiction. She is the author of *Getting Creative with Fab Lab: Creating with Laser Cutters and Engravers* (Rosen Central, 2017), *A Career as a Plumber, Pipefitter, or Steamfitter* (Rosen YA, 2019), as well as several other Rosen career titles. She is coleader of the Kansas City Writers Group and lives in Olathe, Kansas.

PHOTO CREDITS

Design and Layout: Michael Moy; Editor: Bethany Bryan; Photo Researcher: Sherri Jackson